Nos encantan las ciencias
So Into Science!

EXPLOREMOS EL ZOOLÓGICO
EXPLORING THE ZOO

Emmett Martin
Traducido por / Translated by Eida de la Vega

Gareth Stevens PUBLISHING

Please visit our website, www.garethstevens.com. For a free color catalog of all our high-quality books, call toll free 1-800-542-2595 or fax 1-877-542-2596.

Cataloging-in-Publication Data

Names: Martin, Emmett.
Title: Exploring the zoo = Exploremos el zoológico / Emmett Martin.
Description: New York : Gareth Stevens Publishing, 2019. | Series: So into science! = Nos encantan las ciencias | Includes glossary and index.
Identifiers: ISBN 9781538236260 (library bound)
Subjects: LCSH: Zoos–Juvenile literature.
Classification: LCC QL76.M369 2019 | DDC 590.73–dc23

Published in 2019 by
Gareth Stevens Publishing
111 East 14th Street, Suite 349
New York, NY 10003

Translator: Eida de la Vega
Editor, English: Therese Shea
Designer: Sarah Liddell

Photo credits: Cover, p. 1 Thaninee Chuensomchit/Shutterstock.com; p. 5 Trong Nguyen/Shutterstock.com; p. 7 OLJ Studio/Shutterstock.com; p. 9 Rawpixel.com/Shutterstock.com; p. 11 Evikka/Shutterstock.com; pp. 13, 24 (trunk) Q-lieb-in/Shutterstock.com; pp. 15, 24 (mane) Jrossphoto/Shutterstock.com; p. 17 TigerStock's/Shutterstock.com; pp. 19, 24 (parrot) Max3105/Shutterstock.com; p. 21 photobeginner/Shutterstock.com; p. 23 FamVeld/Shutterstock.com.

Printed in the United States of America

CPSIA compliance information: Batch #CW19GS: For further information contact Gareth Stevens, New York, New York at 1-800-542-2595.

Contenido

Contents

¡Hoy vamos
al zoológico!
Puedes ver muchos
animales en el zoológico.

....

We're going
to the zoo today!
You can see many
animals at the zoo.

ZOO
ENTRANCE
NOW OPEN
PURCHASE TICKETS HERE
BUY TICKETS
6 OPEN
8 OPEN
GATE 10

Pagamos para ingresar.

We pay money to go in.

Primero, miramos
el mapa.
Nos dice adónde ir.

....

First, we look
at a map.
It tells us where to go.

ZOO
Tiger
Elephant
Lion
Zoo Shop
Butterfly
Bug
Gibbon
Animal Adventure
Alpaca
Picnic
Pavilion
Sheep
Flamingos
Playground
Garden Hall
Penguin
Aquarium
Entrance
ATTRACTIONS
Kids Adventure

Lo primero que vemos
son los monos.
Un guardián
nos cuenta sobre ellos.

....

We see
the monkeys first.
A zookeeper tells us
about them.

Vemos un elefante.
Rocía agua
con su trompa.

We see an elephant.
It sprays water
with its trunk.

Vemos un león.
Tiene melena,
¡así que es macho!

....

We see a lion.
It has a mane,
so it's a boy!

Vemos un tigre.
Los tigres son
los felinos más grandes.

....

We see a tiger.
Tigers are
the biggest cats!

Vemos aves.
¡Un loro se posa en
el brazo de mi hermana!

We see birds.
A parrot sat on
my sister's arm!

Vemos una jirafa bebé.
¡Es muy alta!

We see a baby giraffe.
It's very tall!

¡Aprendí mucho
en el zoológico!

I learned so much
at the zoo!

Palabras que debes aprender
Words to Know

(el) león
lion

(el) loro
parrot

(la) trompa
trunk

Índice / Index